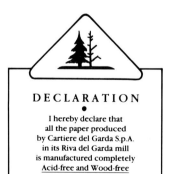

DECLARATION
•

I hereby declare that
all the paper produced
by Cartiere del Garda S.p.A.
in its Riva del Garda mill
is manufactured completely
<u>Acid-free and Wood-free</u>

Dr. Alois Lueftinger
Managing Director and General Manager
Cartiere del Garda S.p.A.

GREEN WORLD

MOSSES
AND LIVERWORTS

Written by
Theresa Greenaway

STECK-VAUGHN
L I B R A R Y
A Division of Steck-Vaughn Company

Austin, Texas

Editor: Wendy Madgwick
Designer: Jane Hunt
Illustrator: Rosie Vane-Wright

Notes to Reader
There are some words in this book that are printed in **bold** type.
A brief explanation of these words is given in the glossary on p. 44.

All living things are given two Latin names when first classified by a
scientist. Some of them also have a common name, for example, the
mountain moss, *Andreaea rupestris*. In this book, the common name is used
where possible, but the scientific name is given when first mentioned.

Library of Congress Cataloging-in-Publication Data
Greenaway, Theresa, 1947–
Mosses and liverworts / written by Theresa Greenaway.
p. cm. – (The Green world)
Includes bibliographical references and index.
Summary: Focuses on varieties and life cycles of mosses and
liverworts in different climates and habitats.
ISBN 0-8114-2738-2
1. Mosses – Juvenile literature.   2. Liverworts – Juvenile literature.
[1. Mosses.   2. Liverworts.]   I. Title.   II. Series
QK5375.G74   1991   91-14936
588–dc20   CIP AC

Color separations by Chroma Graphics, Singapore
Printed and bound by L.E.G.O., Vicenza, Italy
1 2 3 4 5 6 7 8 9 0 LE 96 95 94 93 92

Photographic credits
t = top, b = bottom, l = left, r = right
Cover: Bruce Coleman; page 13 Frank Lane/A. Wilson; page 14
Operation Raleigh/Jon Cook; page 15 Bruce Coleman/F. Sauer;
page 17 Smith/Polunin Collection; page 18 Bruce Coleman/
S.J. Krasemann; page 19 Bruce Coleman/J. & D. Bartlett; page 20
Bruce Coleman/E. Crichton; page 21 Bruce Coleman/E. Crichton;
page 25 Dr Shaun Edwards; page 27*l* Frank Lane/Premaphotos Wildlife;
page 27*r* Frank Lane/A. Wharton; page 28 Bruce Coleman/
K. Taylor; page 29 Bruce Coleman/H. Reinhard; page 31 Bruce
Coleman/Jane Burton; page 32 Bruce Coleman/C. J. Ott; page 34 Frank
Lane/R. Hosking; page 37 Frank Lane/M. L. Van Nostrand;
page 39 Frank Lane/D. T. Grewcock; page 41 Bruce Coleman/
M. Klinec; page 42 The British Museum.

CONTENTS

GREEN WORLD

This tree shows the different groups of plants that are found in the world. It does not show how they developed or their relationship with each other.

CONIFEROUS (OR FIR) TREES (Gymnosperms)

FLOWERING PLANTS (Angiosperms)

FERNS, CLUB MOSSES, AND HORSETAILS (Pteridophytes)

MOSSES AND LIVERWORTS (Bryophytes)

GREEN PLANTS

ALGAE

PLANTS

ANIMALS

FUNGI AND LICHENS

BACTERIA

SLIME MOLDS

LIVING THINGS

Group 1
Liverworts
Thallose liverworts
■ Green plant body flat and lobed, sometimes ribbonlike

Leafy liverworts
■ Stems upright or creeping
■ Stems always leafy
■ Leaves often lobed

Group 2
Mosses
Bogmosses (Sphagnidae)
■ Upright mosses of wet, acid places
■ Capsules round
■ Branches in bunches

Mountain mosses (Andreaeidae)
■ Minute, oval capsules
■ Capsule opens into a miniature "lantern" with four slits

True mosses (Bryidae)
■ Leaves simple, never lobed
■ Capsules oval or oblong, opening by a peristome
■ Stem of sporophyte tough and colored.

The land area of the world is divided into ten main zones depending on the plants that grow there. Mosses and liverworts can be found in most parts of the world except in deserts or in the ocean.

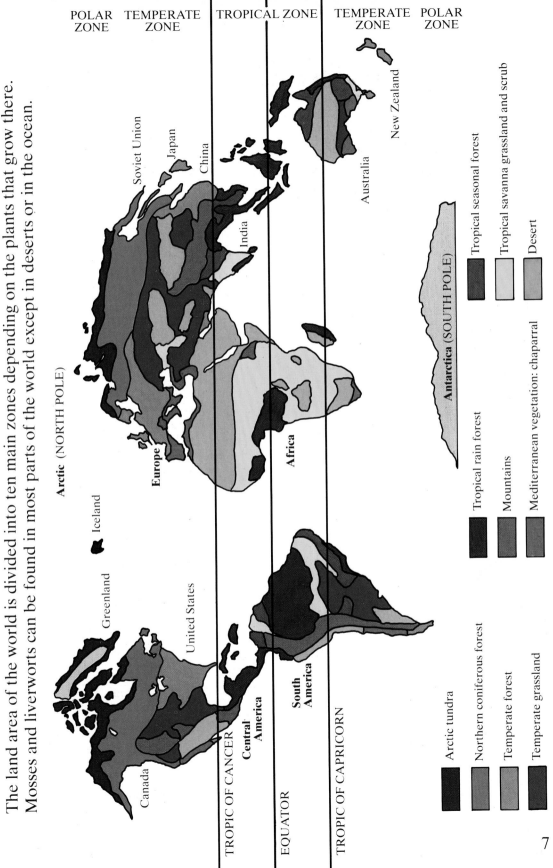

POLAR ZONE TEMPERATE ZONE TROPICAL ZONE TEMPERATE ZONE POLAR ZONE

Arctic (NORTH POLE)

Soviet Union
Japan
China
India
Iceland
Greenland
United States
Canada
Europe
Africa
New Zealand
Australia
Central America
South America
TROPIC OF CANCER
EQUATOR
TROPIC OF CAPRICORN

Antarctica (SOUTH POLE)

Arctic tundra
Northern coniferous forest
Temperate forest
Temperate grassland

Tropical rain forest
Mountains
Mediterranean vegetation: chaparral

Tropical seasonal forest
Tropical savanna grassland and scrub
Desert

7

MOSSES AND LIVERWORTS

osses and liverworts are tiny plants that do not produce flowers. Together they make up the group that botanists (people who study plants) call **bryophytes**. The main feature that separates bryophytes from other groups of plants is that their life cycle has two stages. The leafy plant that you recognize as a moss or liverwort is the first stage, the **gametophyte** (see p. 26). At certain times of the year, a long, stalked **capsule** appears. This is the second stage, the **sporophyte**. Each capsule is filled with minute, dustlike **spores**, each of which can grow into a new plant.

Bryophytes are fairly simple in structure. Their stems, though often tough, are never woody. Their leaves are thin and usually only one cell thick. They have a great many

World distribution

There are about 25,000 species of bryophytes. They are most abundant in damp climates, but mosses and liverworts can be found in nearly all parts of the world except in deserts or in the ocean. Some are limited to particular conditions, but others can grow almost anywhere.

They are usually small; many are between 1 and 4 inches tall. In the warm, moist tropics, they grow larger. Other mosses are very tiny and cannot be seen properly without magnification. Often these very tiny plants grow in a group or colony, making a tuft or a matlike layer that may cover a large area.

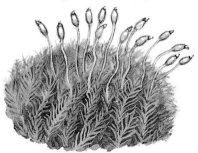

The moss *Distichium capillaceum* only grows on wet, limestone rocks.

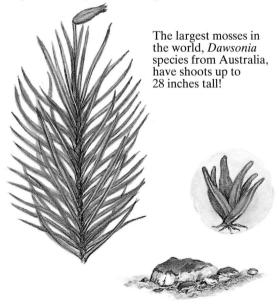

The largest mosses in the world, *Dawsonia* species from Australia, have shoots up to 28 inches tall!

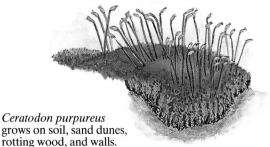

Ceratodon purpureus grows on soil, sand dunes, rotting wood, and walls.

In *Seligeria calcarea*, each tiny moss plant is only about .04 inch tall, but thousands grow so closely together that they completely cover chalky rocks.

leaves, which grow along the length of the thin stem. Some liverworts, however, do not have leaves. These liverworts have a flat, ribbonlike, or lobed plant body called a **thallus**. Bryophytes do not have actual roots; instead, they are anchored to the ground by tiny, fine rootlets known as **rhizoids** (see p. 22).

Many kinds, or species, can only grow in wet or damp places because their leaves are so thin that they dry out very easily. Also, all mosses and liverworts need moisture to reproduce and form new plants (see p. 27).

Mosses and liverworts contain the green pigment **chlorophyll** used with the energy in sunlight to make sugars from carbon dioxide gas and water. This process is called **photosynthesis**, and is the way that all green plants make their food.

■ Mosses and liverworts are small green plants belonging to the Bryophyta.
■ They either have a leafy stem (most mosses and liverworts) or a flat, lobed body called a thallus (some liverworts).
■ The plant is anchored to the ground by rhizoids.
■ All grow in moist places and are found throughout the world.

Mnium hornum is a leafy moss found in woodlands.

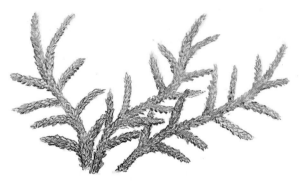

Pseudoscleropodium purum is a leafy moss from North America, Europe, and Asia.

Sphagnum rubellum is a red bog moss from northern bogs.

Lunularia cruciata is a thallose liverwort found around the world.

Plagiochila asplenioides is a leafy liverwort of moist, shady places.

MOSS OR LIVERWORT?

Bryophytes first evolved about 390 million years ago, in the Silurian period. They were among the very first land plants. The first air-breathing creatures like scorpions and millipedes appeared at the same time.

Most people know what mosses are, but very few can identify, or tell the difference between, the many species. This is partly because neither mosses nor liverworts have flowers to help in their identification. The main reason, however, is that they are so small. In order to study the shape of the leaves, capsules, and male or female parts (see p. 26), a magnifying glass or even a microscope is needed. People who study mosses and liverworts are called **bryologists**.

Liverworts

In general, liverworts need damper surroundings than mosses, and so they grow in fewer **habitats**. Liverworts can be divided into two groups; those with leaves and those with a flat, thallose plant body. There are many more leafy liverworts than thallose liverworts.

leafy liverwort, *Bazzania trilobata*

thallose liverwort, *Conocephalum conicum*

Moss or Liverwort?

■ Most liverworts have leaves arranged in three rows – one row down each side of the stem and a third row of tiny leaves hidden below these on the underside of the stem. Most moss leaves grow all around the stem.

■ Moss leaves often have a midrib, or vein. Liverwort leaves never have midribs.

■ Liverwort capsules are carried on weak, colorless stalks. Moss capsules are on thin but wiry stalks that are often orange, red, or yellow.

■ Liverwort capsules are mostly round and split into four parts when ripe. Moss capsules are oval or oblong. When they are ripe the lid falls off, and a row of teeth opens to release the spores. Bogmosses are an exception, and have round capsules like liverworts.

Mosses

Mosses can be divided into two main groups, the bogmosses (*Sphagnum* species) and true mosses. There is also another very small group of mountain mosses (*Andreaea* species).

There are over 300 species of bogmosses. They are all acid-loving plants that live in very wet, peaty places or slow streams.

The true mosses are the largest group of bryophytes. They are very varied in size and appearance and grow in very different places. For instance, some will only grow on bare soil. Others grow in very shady places, while others are only found on tree leaves or tree trunks. It is possible to find out quite a lot about an environment from the kinds of mosses growing there.

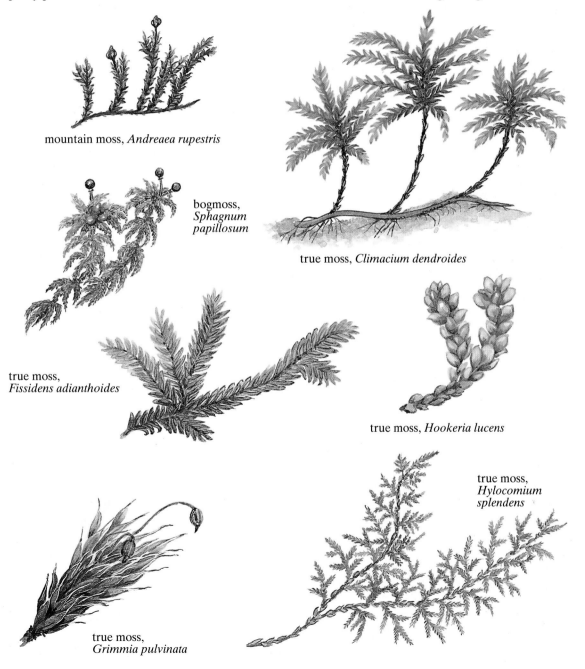

mountain moss, *Andreaea rupestris*

bogmoss, *Sphagnum papillosum*

true moss, *Climacium dendroides*

true moss, *Fissidens adianthoides*

true moss, *Hookeria lucens*

true moss, *Hylocomium splendens*

true moss, *Grimmia pulvinata*

MOSSES OF WET PLACES

Bogs are wet, treeless places. They are found in cool, temperate regions with a high rainfall, or on high mountain slopes in the tropics. The waterlogged soil is peaty and acid, with only small amounts of plant nutrients.

A raised bog begins as a low-lying, flat, badly drained area lashed by rain. Over the years, it builds up into a dome of **peat** with a layer of sphagnum and other bog plants covering it. Blanket bogs cover wet, upland slopes, although they can be found at sea level, too. North America, Ireland, Scotland, northwest England, northern Europe, Finland, and the Soviet Union all have large areas of bog. In the south, the southerly tips of South America and South Island, New Zealand, have the largest bogs.

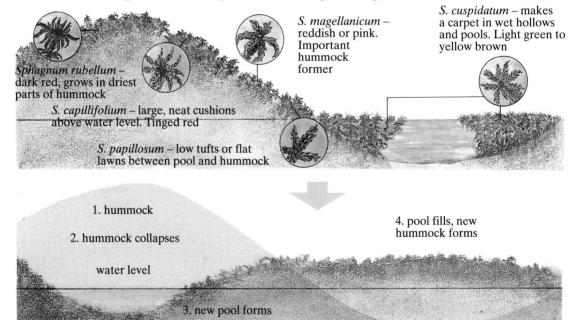

S. magellanicum – reddish or pink. Important hummock former

S. cuspidatum – makes a carpet in wet hollows and pools. Light green to yellow brown

Sphagnum rubellum – dark red, grows in driest parts of hummock

S. capillifolium – large, neat cushions above water level. Tinged red

S. papillosum – low tufts or flat lawns between pool and hummock

1. hummock

2. hummock collapses

water level

3. new pool forms

4. pool fills, new hummock forms

Sphagnum bogs

Sphagnum bogs are made up of lots of small mounds, or hummocks, separated by hollows which are often filled with water (see above). Different species of *Sphagnum* grow in the hummocks and hollows, each occupying a particular **niche**. As the bogmosses grow upward and outward, the hollows fill with the most aquatic (water-loving) of sphagnum mosses. Species that prefer slightly drier edges of the pool gradually spread into the center as the water disappears. At the same time, bogmosses at the top of the hummocks grow too far away from the water and become too dry. The sphagnum moss dies and the center of the hummock collapses, making a new hollow that fills with water.

Freshwater mosses and liverworts

Lots of mosses and liverworts grow close to water. It may be only a trickle from a leaking pipe, a splash from a waterfall, or moist rocks beside a stream. A few grow below the water surface.

Unlike a bog, running water contains a lot of oxygen and often carries dissolved nutrients. All these bryophytes, as well as those that grow around the margins of pools and lakes, provide shelter for tiny water creatures.

Fontinalis antipyretica, a moss, is common in slow-flowing rivers, lakes, and ponds. It is a leafy, dark green moss with branches that may be as long as 28 inches.

The liverwort *Riccia fluitans* floats on the surface of ponds and ditches.

The mosses *Cinclidotus fontinaloides* and *Eurynchium riparioides* also prefer the swiftly moving water of rivers and streams.

Another liverwort, *Scapania undulata*, is reddish-purple in color and grows in large patches in fast-moving streams.

Coastal mosses

No mosses can live in the sea, but a few are found on rocks along beaches, where they are splashed at high tide. These include *Grimmia maritima* (see below) and *Ulota phyllantha*.

Mosses That Are Not Mosses

When is a moss not a moss?
None of these is a moss!

Carrageen moss is a red seaweed.

Iceland moss is a lichen.

Reindeer moss is another lichen.

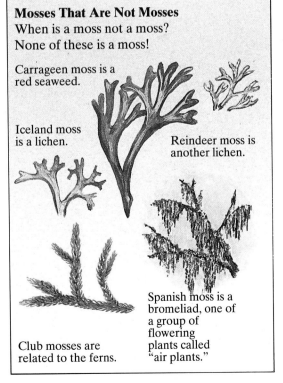

Club mosses are related to the ferns.

Spanish moss is a bromeliad, one of a group of flowering plants called "air plants."

TROPICAL BRYOPHYTES

Tropical rain forests are found on low-lying land near the equator in Africa, Asia, South and Central America, and Queensland, Australia. These forests are made up of huge trees, often with massive trunks. The forest canopy is about 90 feet high, although taller trees can reach over 120 feet. There are also woody climbing plants called lianas. The dense, evergreen foliage of the canopy shades out much of the light, so very little vegetation can grow on the forest floor.

The leaves of tropical rain forest trees are often large, and they may live for a long time before falling. High in the canopy it is brighter, and many mosses and liverworts grow as **epiphytes** on the leaves, twigs, and branches. Ferns, lichens, and special kinds of flowering plants are also found there.

Among the branches
Numerous kinds of mosses and leafy liverworts live on the tree leaves and branches (see right). Probably many species have yet to be discovered.

These tiny plants, together with all the other epiphytes, trap water as well as bits of dead plants, insects, and animal droppings. These are broken down by microorganisms (microscopic living things), and the nutrients they contain are recycled high above the forest floor. Sometimes even the tree itself grows tiny roots from its twigs into these "compost heaps."

Montane forests

Tropical rain forest is a lowland forest. Higher up on the slopes of mountains in the tropics, between about 3,300 and 8,200 feet, there is another kind of wet forest. This is called the montane or mossy forest. Montane forests are found in Asia, on the tropical slopes of the Andes, on mountain regions of the West Indies, and in Africa (see below). The climate is cooler than at lower altitudes. Because of the almost permanent mists and low clouds, it is not very sunny, and moisture does not evaporate from the vegetation. The soils are acid and poor in nutrients, somewhat like peat bogs.

The trees in the montane forests are much shorter, and so the forest canopy forms at about 20 feet, much lower than a lowland rain forest. However, it is difficult to see montane forest trees clearly because they are smothered with a thick layer of mosses and leafy liverworts. The growth of epiphytes is so luxuriant that each tree trunk looks twice as thick as it really is.

The forest floor

The ground in montane forests is covered with ferns, mosses, and bamboos. *Dawsonia superba* grows on the forest floor. This is such a large moss that it can be mistaken for a pine-tree seedling! *Spiridens* is a spectacular moss that grows on tree fern trunks. Another impressive moss is *Pterobryella papuensis*, which has fronds the size of ferns.

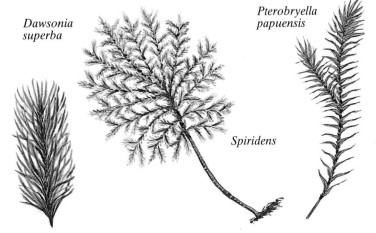

Dawsonia superba

Pterobryella papuensis

Spiridens

15

TEMPERATE WOODLANDS

Woods in temperate parts of the world have a cooler climate than tropical forests and are usually much drier. The seasons are more distinct. Summers are warm, but winters are cold, often with frost or snow. The trees that grow there, for example oak and ash, are deciduous – that is, their leaves fall in autumn. These leaves break down to form a rich compost. Wild flowers and shrubs grow well, but mosses are still important. They are easy to see in winter, when the trees are bare.

Huge forests of conifers (spruces, pines, and larches) grow across northern Canada and northern Europe and Asia. Near the sea these forests are quite wet, but farther inland there may be little rainfall. The forest floor is so dark that wild flowers and shrubs cannot grow there. Mosses and liverworts can survive, however. Conifers are evergreen and do not shed all their leaves in autumn. They are shed throughout the year. The conifer needles rot slowly and produce an acid leaf litter lacking in nutrients.

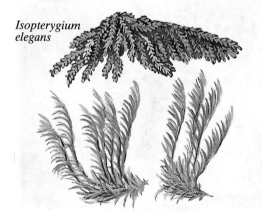

Isopterygium elegans

Eurynchium praelongum

Brachythecium rutabulum

Dicranum scoparium

Worldwide mosses

Mosses are an ancient group of plants; they also have exceedingly light spores that can travel long distances in the air. For these reasons, there is less difference between the mosses of the same kinds of habitat on different continents than among the wild flowers. Therefore the deciduous woodlands of the eastern U.S. have very similar, and often identical, mosses to European and British woods. *Isopterygium elegans*, *Eurynchium praelongum*, *Dicranum scoparium*, and *Brachythecium rutabulum* are abundant in both (see above). Sometimes, there are pairs of very similar mosses, for example *Rhynchostegium serratum* in North America and *R. confertum* in Europe.

Temperate rain forests

The mild, damp forests of the western coastal strip of North America, the tip of South America, and New Zealand abound with bryophytes. New Zealand is particularly rich in both mosses and liverworts, and 30 species are found nowhere else in the world.

Chalk-lovers

The European beech often grows on very chalky ground. A characteristic chalk-loving moss of beechwoods is *Cirriphyllum crassinervium*, and the liverwort *Porella platyphylla* flourishes in damper patches (see below).

Neohodgsonia mirabilis

Pulchrinodus inflatus

Cirriphyllum crassinervium

Porella platyphylla

Coniferous forests

A thick blanket of creeping mosses covers the ground, fallen branches, and tree stumps in coniferous forests (see right). *Pleurozium schreberi* and *Hylocomium splendens* are two of the most widespread species. In the drier areas, *Polytrichum* species, *Dicranum* species, and *Ceratodon purpureus* are among the mosses most often seen. *Sphagnum* mosses grow in wetter areas, together with *Aulacomnium palustre* and *Mnium* species.

BRYOPHYTES OF THE COLD

The most northerly parts of North America, Europe, and the Soviet Union make up the arctic **tundra**. Beyond it is a permanent cap of sea ice – the frozen Arctic Ocean. The arctic climate is severe, with long, dark, and very cold winters. In the southern parts of the tundra, summer temperatures may reach 70°F, but in general the summer is cool and brief.

The land is frozen for much of the year, and even in summer only the top layer thaws. The ice-bound ground below is known as the **permafrost**. Much of the tundra has surprisingly little rain or snowfall because cold air cannot hold much moisture. When the soil surface thaws, the water cannot drain away through the permafrost, so the land becomes marshy.

The tundra landscape is molded by repeated freezing and thawing, resulting in many peculiar features. One of these is the distinctive ground pattern of polygonal shapes. As the ground freezes in early winter, it shrinks and cracks into **polygons**. In summer, melting ice fills the cracks. Next winter, the ground freezes and contracts again, and the ice wedge expands, widening the cracks. Many mosses and liverworts grow in these cracks or crevices.

Plants of the tundra

The plants of the tundra (see above) have to survive icy winds, extremely low temperatures, and a short growing season. The soils are often thin and infertile. Trees cannot grow at all. Many low-growing flowering plants are found in the southern parts of the tundra, covering the ground with color during their brief flowering season. Mosses also grow well there, including sphagnum moss, which grows in the wettest places and around lakes.

Plants of ice and snow

Farther north there are fewer and fewer flowering plants. Instead, lichens and mosses make up the vegetation. Some mosses are found only in the arctic tundra, but many are found on cold mountaintops and on the islands around Antarctica. These include *Rhacomitrium lanuginosum*, *Ditrichum flexicaule*, and *Drepanocladus uncinatus*.

In the dry polar deserts, most of the mosses and a few liverworts live in the damper, more protected crevices of the polygons. The liverwort plants are tiny. Those such as *Cephaloziella arctica* and *Lophozia* look like a blackish patch on the ground.

Rhacomitrium lanuginosum

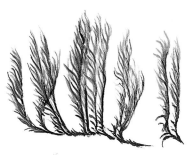

Ditrichum flexicaule

Drepanocladus uncinatus

Cephaloziella arctica

Antarctica

Unlike the Arctic, Antarctica is a frozen continent covered with ice and snow. There is virtually no plant life on the continent itself – just a few tiny algae, fungi, and lichens trapped in frozen rock. The climate of the South Orkney Islands is less harsh. Lichens, mosses, and fungi are found there, but growth is very, very slow. Farther north, the South Georgia Islands (see left) support ferns and flowering plants, as well as mosses, including sphagnum, and lichens.

19

ARTIFICIAL HABITATS

Tiny villages, industrial sites, large cities, roads, bridges, schools, and churches all have something in common. They all have large areas of bare brickwork, stone, masonry, or concrete. In fact, they are artificial cliffs or rocky slopes. Many building materials contain lime or chalk and, like natural rocks, are often quite dry, especially in the summer.

Some kinds of mosses can stand long periods without moisture. They are the **ectohydric** mosses (see p. 30), which absorb water from the air. In the wild, they live in dry places, often on south-facing slopes and craggy outcrops. Some of these drought-tolerant mosses have moved from the country into the town, where they have colonized walls, roofs, and pathways. A few thrive so well that they are now more common in their new homes than in their natural environment! In order to flourish in urban surroundings, these mosses have to be able to tolerate dirt and pollutants in the air.

Town mosses

Bryum argenteum, Tortula muralis, and *Grimmia pulvinata* (see above) are very tolerant of the dirt and pollution that are part of city life. All three of these mosses are common on brick and stone walls. *Bryum argenteum* can grow where very few other plants succeed – in the cracks between paving stones. *Orthotrichum diaphanum* is another "town" moss that lives on damp walls and pavements. The success of these mosses may be due partly to a plentiful supply of nutrients in the waste from dogs and city birds.

Vacant lots

Rhacomitrium canescens, shown below, is a moss of sandy and gravelly soils and heaths. It grows into a grayish, rough-looking mat that can withstand desiccation (drying out) in hot summer sunshine, when it is crunchy to walk on. It has successfully colonized sandy vacant lots, rural roadsides, and gravel paths.

Greenhouses

Gardeners keep their plants in a warm, humid greenhouse and grow them in a fertile compost. These are ideal conditions for the growth of many bryophytes, but two liverworts in particular, *Lunularia cruciata* and *Marchantia polymorpha*, thrive there. They grow on the compost at the base of the potted plants (see below).

Mosses in lawns and pastures

Lawns and grazed grasslands are just as artificial as buildings and pavements. In temperate parts of North America, Asia, and Europe, much of the land that is now built on or farmed was once woodland. The grass of pastures is kept short by domestic animals. Lawns, playing fields, and parks are kept short by using mechanical grazers – mowers. Some mosses grow well in short turf, especially when it is overgrazed. Too much mowing has the same effect as heavy grazing. The grass cover wears thin, and mosses invade. One such moss is *Rhytidiadelphus squarrosus*, shown on the right.

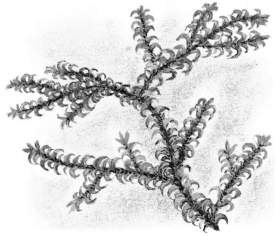

MOSSES: SHAPE AND FORM

When a moss spore settles in a suitably damp spot, it germinates and begins to grow. First, a very tiny threadlike plant, the **protonema**, appears. After a while buds develop and each of these grows into a moss plant.

A moss plant has a thin, often tough, stem with numerous leaves. Many mosses have tiny rootlets, or rhizoids, but some only have these in the young plant. Rhizoids look like fine brown hairs. They hold the plant firmly onto the rock, tree trunk, or soil on which it is growing. Some mosses also absorb water through their rhizoids. At certain times most mosses produce capsules (see p. 29).

All true mosses are leafy. The leaves are usually arranged more or less spirally around the stem, although *Fissidens* species have leaves in rows. Moss leaves are small and stalkless. Some have one midrib, or vein, a few have two short veins, and some have none at all. The leaf blade, or lamina, is only one cell thick in most mosses, but bogmosses and *Leucobryum* species have thicker leaf blades.

The basic plan
Mosses such as *Funaria* have straight, unbranched stems, but many other kinds are branched. The stems are very simple in construction and, unlike the stems of flowering plants, they are not made up of different types of cells, or building blocks. Mosses grow to form different kinds of clumps : wefts (*Thuidium tamariscinum*), mats (*Hypnum cupressiforme*), or cushions (*Leucobryum glaucum*).

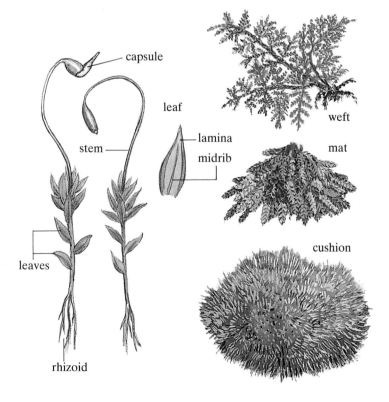

capsule

leaf

stem

lamina

midrib

leaves

rhizoid

weft

mat

cushion

The bogmosses

Sphagnum mosses are found on wet ground. A sphagnum spore germinates to make a tiny, platelike protonema, which grows into single plant. The stems are weak, but lots of plants grow together in a clump, and they support each other. Mosses grow only from the tips of the plants, where new leaves or branches are continually formed. Older parts of the stem just die and rot away; there are no rhizoids.

Sphagnum branches are usually in bunches of five. In each bunch, some stick out; the rest grow downward and cover the stem. The short branches are covered with tiny leaves.

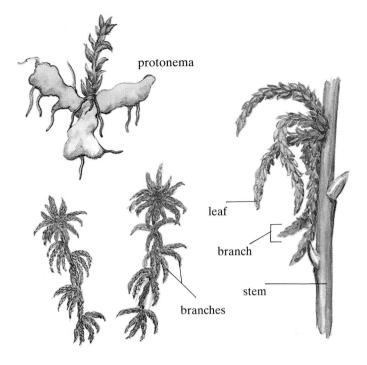

protonema

leaf

branch

stem

branches

No midribs

The leaves of bogmosses do not have midribs. They are made of a network of thin, green cells sandwiched between much larger clear cells. The walls of these larger cells have tiny pores, or holes, through which water can be absorbed. These cells enable sphagnum plants to behave like sponges, soaking up large amounts of water. Some species are pink or red.

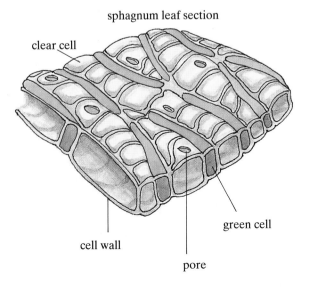

sphagnum leaf section

clear cell

cell wall

pore

green cell

Leaf Shapes

Moss leaves are simple in shape and are never divided into smaller leaflets or lobes. Some have very finely toothed margins; others have smooth edges. Some have twisted leaves. Many mosses have the leaf tips drawn out into a long, fine point. These points are colorless, which gives the moss a "frosted" look.

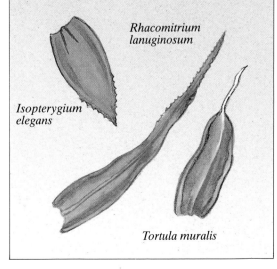

Rhacomitrium lanuginosum

Isopterygium elegans

Tortula muralis

THE SHAPE OF LIVERWORTS

Thallose liverworts are very easily recognized because no other land plants are flat and bright green. Some lichens are flat and lobed, but they are mostly brown, grayish, or yellow. "Liverworts" get their name from the resemblance of their lobed appearance to an animal's lobed liver – but here the likeness ends!

Some thallose liverworts such as *Riccia* are extremely simple inside, but *Marchantia* is much more complex. Its surface is covered by a waterproof **cuticle**, or skin. Moisture and gases can enter through pores, or holes, in the cuticle. Inside the thallus there are air chambers, and each lobe has a faint midrib.

Leafy liverworts also have tiny, one-celled rhizoids. Their stems sometimes grow upright, but often creep over the surface of the ground or tree where they are growing. They appear either as tufts or as a **weft** of stems (see right). They can be bright green, red, purple, yellow, or black. Their leaves are in two or three rows along the stem. Two rows grow laterally (to the side), at each side of the stem. Sometimes a third row of much smaller leaves grow underneath the stem. The leaves of liverworts are stalkless and very thin.

Thallose liverworts
A thallose liverwort spore germinates into a tiny protonema that eventually makes one bud. Species of *Marchantia* are common in many parts of the world. The thallus is darkish green. It is like a ribbon that has branched dichotomously (into two even halves) many times. Eventually, it looks like a lobed green mat (see right). On the lower surface, there are many tiny rhizoids, each consisting of only one cell. These rhizoids anchor the plant to the ground.

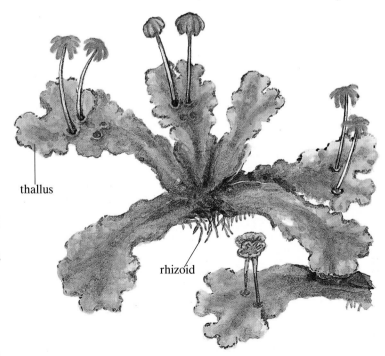

thallus

rhizoid

Leafy liverworts

The leaves of liverworts never have veins. Their side leaves are often toothed or lobed. Sometimes the lobes are twisted around so it looks as though there are five rows of leaves. Some liverworts have leaves that overlap and cup the stem so closely that the separate rows cannot be seen at all. Leafy liverworts grow in different ways. Some form leafy tufts (*Bazzania trilobata*); others grow close to the ground, forming dense mats (*Frullania dilatata*) or looser spreading wefts (*Lophocolea heterophylla*).

Bazzania trilobata

Frullania dilatata

Lophocolea heterophylla

Hornworts

These are a small group usually included with the liverworts. Like the thallose liverworts, they have a green plant body. They are called "hornworts" because they have long capsules that grow up from the thallus like curved horns. *Anthoceros* (shown left) is a hornwort with so many lobes that the edge of the plant is very wavy. It grows on damp rocks and wet soil. Inside the thallus there are chambers similar to those seen in *Marchantia*, but instead of air, they are filled with slimy mucilage (jelly).

25

LIFE CYCLES

The life cycle of bryophytes, both mosses and liverworts, is made up of two distinct stages, each called a **generation**. The green plant we recognize as the moss or liverwort is the gametophyte generation. This stage produces the male and female sex organs that produce the male and female sex cells, or **gametes**. The other stage is the sporophyte generation, which produces a capsule that contains the spores that grow into new gametophyte plants.

The female sex organ, an **archegonium**, is a microscopic, long-necked flask. Each one contains a single sex cell or egg. When ripe, each male organ, an **antheridium**, releases a large number of male sex cells, called **zoospores**. Each of these is very tiny and has two tails, or **flagella**. In order to fertilize the female sex cell, the zoospore has to swim to a ripe archegonium. It can do this only when the plant is wet.

Zoospores are attracted to the tiny neck of a ripe archegonium by special chemicals. After entering, it unites with, or **fertilizes**, the female sex cell. This is **sexual reproduction**. The fertilized egg immediately begins to grow and develops into a sporophyte. The sporophyte cannot live by itself; it grows on the gametophyte plant.

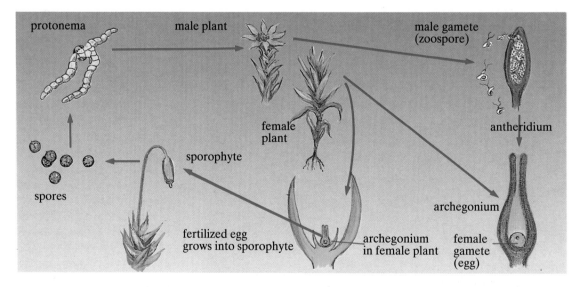

Alternation of generations
The life cycle of bryophytes (gametophyte→ sporophyte→ gametophyte→ sporophyte) is known as alternation of generations. It is this life cycle that makes the bryophytes different from all other groups of plants.

Moss antheridia and archegonia

Groups of antheridia (see below) and archegonia are often surrounded by rosettes of leaves. These round antheridia may be bright red or orange. At first glance they could be mistaken for tiny flowers. Archegonia are hidden inside a cup of leaves.

Liverwort antheridia and archegonia

The sex organs of *Marchantia* (see below) are borne on "umbrellas" that grow on stalks from the edge of the thallus. Antheridia grow on the top and archegonia on the underside. Leafy liverworts have their sex organs singly or in small groups in the **axils** of special leaves.

Sporophyte stages

Moss sporophytes are varied in shape, size, and color, and can be used to help identify the different species. Each has a foot, a thin stem or **seta**, and a capsule. Stems are often tall and hold the capsule well above the moss plant. Some capsules have a thin hood, or **calyptra**. This is the remains of the archegonium.

Liverwort sporophytes show less variety in shape than moss sporophytes. The stems are short, weak, and pale green. The capsule appears from below the "umbrella" in *Marchantia*. In leafy liverworts, the capsule emerges from the top of the **perianth**.

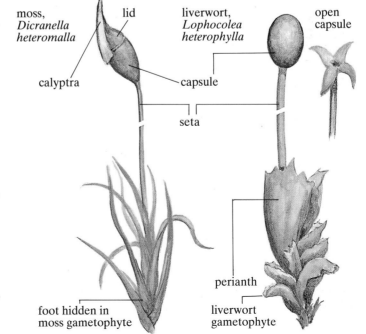

moss, *Dicranella heteromalla*

lid

calyptra

capsule

liverwort, *Lophocolea heterophylla*

open capsule

seta

perianth

foot hidden in moss gametophyte

liverwort gametophyte

27

MAKING NEW PLANTS

Moss capsules are very noticeable because they all appear on the same moss clump at the same time. Ripe capsules are full of thousands of powdery spores. Beneath the lid is the **peristome**, which is made up of one or two rows of "teeth" that vary in length, shape, and number. They are often used to identify a moss. Peristome teeth are very sensitive to changes in humidity (the moisture content of the air). When the air is dry, the teeth bend out and twist in such a way that the capsule opens and some of the spores are flicked out. When the air becomes damp, the teeth can twist back to close the capsule.

The spores are wafted away and spread by air currents. If they land in a place with moisture and nutrients, they can germinate and grow.

Bogmosses have round capsules. When the capsules dry in the sun, they explode, forcing off their lids. If you listen very carefully, you can hear the sound that it makes. The "explosion" shoots out the spores, which are blown away by the wind.

Gemmae

Bryophytes also spread by means of **gemmae** (see right). These are small, budlike outgrowths consisting of a few green cells. They often develop along the edges of the leaves. When they are mature, they fall off and grow into new plants.

The liverwort *Marchantia* has gemmae that develop in a little green cup on the upper surface of the thallus. They look like minute green eggs in a tiny nest. When it rains, the cup fills with water, which loosens the gemmae. As raindrops splash into the cup, the spores are washed out onto bare soil where they germinate and grow.

Moss capsules

Moss capsules contain thousands of tiny spores. When these are ripe, the lid falls off and the peristome teeth open out to release the spores.

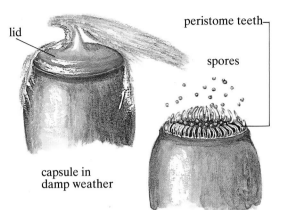

lid

peristome teeth

spores

capsule in damp weather

capsule in dry weather

Liverworts

The capsules of liverworts do not have lids or peristome teeth. Instead, when the capsules are ripe, they split into four sections, and the spores are shaken out by air movements (see below).

Asexual Reproduction

Besides reproducing sexually, bryophytes also increase their numbers vegetatively. This does not involve the uniting of sex cells and so is called asexual reproduction. Some mosses are infertile: they never have a sporophyte generation, and are always spread by asexual means.

If a small piece of moss is broken off, it can sprout rhizoids and grow into a new plant. Some kinds of leafy liverworts, especially tropical species, have leaves or branches that break off very readily. They are dispersed by raindrops, and each may grow into another liverwort plant. As the older parts of a weft-forming moss die away, all the younger branches can grow into new plants.

Pleurozium schreberi

year 1

year 2
two or more
new plants
made

older parts die

FOOD AND WATER

Mosses and liverworts make their food by photo-synthesis. The energy in sunlight activates the molecules of the green pigment chlorophyll. This sets off a chain of chemical reactions in which carbon dioxide gas and water are combined to make simple sugars.

Water is also essential. Mosses and liverworts can take up water in two ways. Some have rhizoids that can absorb water from the ground. They are called **endohydric** mosses and include the hair mosses, *Polytrichum* species. Liverworts related to *Marchantia* are also endohydric. The leaf surface of endohydric mosses, and the upper surface of the *Marchantia* thallus, are covered with a thin waterproof layer, the cuticle. This stops water from being lost through evaporation.

Most mosses and leafy liverworts have rhizoids that do not absorb water, or no rhizoids at all, like bogmosses. They absorb water, nutrients, and minerals from rain, dew, or mist directly through their leaves, which do not have a waterproof cuticle. These mosses and liverworts are ectohydric. Their leaves are arranged to trap and hold water droplets.

Water and food absorption
Water and essential nutrients are taken up by rhizoids in endohydric mosses and liverworts. In ectohydric bryophytes they are taken in through the leaves (see below).

endohydric moss,
Polytrichum commune

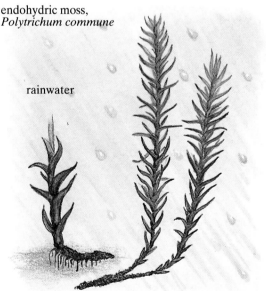

rainwater

water absorbed by rhizoids

ectohydric moss,
Grimmia pulvinata

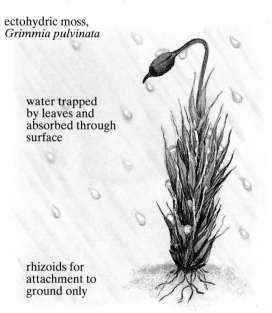

water trapped by leaves and absorbed through surface

rhizoids for attachment to ground only

Survival in drought

Some ectohydric mosses can survive for weeks in a completely dried-out state (see left). When rain finally falls, they recover quickly, none the worse for wear. These are the kinds of mosses that live in places likely to dry out in summer – walls, heaths, and dry banks.

Bogmosses

You might think that bogs are such soggy wet places that bogmosses have no need to save water, but there is little shade on a treeless bog, and the sun can be hot. To keep the moss from drying out, rainwater and groundwater are soaked up and held in special water-holding cells in the leaves.

Bogs are not very fertile places for plants to grow. As bogs are acid, the normal processes of decay are slow, so minerals stay locked up in the remains of dead plants. The water comes largely from rain and supplies few nutrients. *Sphagnum* plants are able to "scavenge" scarce but vital nutrients. Chemicals in their cell walls exchange minerals in the water for hydrogen ions (part of the water molecule often written as H^+) from the plant itself. The release of H^+ ions into the surrounding water actually increases the acidity of the bog, as "acidity" is a measure of the H^+ content of watery places.

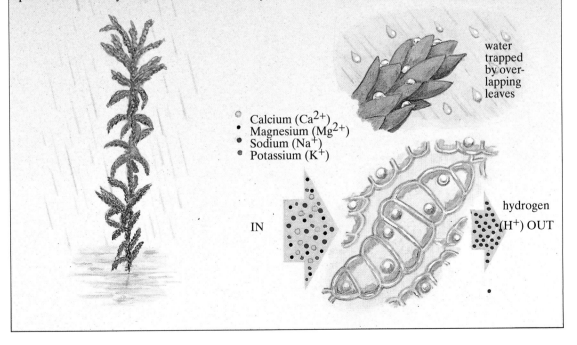

water trapped by over-lapping leaves

Calcium (Ca^{2+})
Magnesium (Mg^{2+})
Sodium (Na^+)
Potassium (K^+)

IN

hydrogen (H^+) OUT

THE COLONIZERS

Even before people began clearing land to farm or build, natural disasters such as fires, floods, avalanches, or earthquakes exposed soil, rocks, or burned earth. It is difficult for plants to grow on recently disturbed ground because the surface may be loose and move easily. Rainwater drains away too quickly, leaving the soil dry. Freshly bared rocks are either too dry or too wet, and rain washes away seedlings. It takes a long time for the original vegetation to return.

The first plants to grow on bare ground are called **primary colonizers**. As the plants grow, they bind together and **stabilize** the soil surface so that it is not washed or blown away. Gradually different plants begin to grow there.

This series is called a **succession**. Mosses are often important in the early stages of a succession. Their light spores are carried in the air and soon settle. Spreading mosses hold the loose soil and trap water, so small flowering plants can take root.

Bryum pendulum   *Tortula ruraliformis*

Sand dunes

The seaward edge of coastal sand dunes is built up by the action of the wind. Fresh loose sand often buries colonizing plants. Farther back, the dune surface becomes stabilized by an increasingly thick mat of vegetation. One of the most important plants of sand dunes is marram grass, but mosses are also an important feature of dunes (see above).

Nothing wasted

In nature, nothing is left bare for long. *Splachnum* mosses grow on sheep or cattle dung (see above). They are tiny mosses but are easily seen because they produce a dense forest of sporophytes with small, distinctive capsules. A Scandinavian species of *Splachnum* has a smell that attracts dung flies. The spores cling to the fly, who then plants them on fresh dung!

Mountain screes

Avalanches and rock falls on mountainsides result in the steep slopes of loose, rocky rubble called screes. They are unstable and difficult to walk on. Mosses and liverworts grow in the damp, shaded cracks between the stones and, in time, cover and help to stabilize the scree, allowing other plants to become established.

Mountain scree succession

bare rocks

Grimmia on tops of rocks

Rhacomitrium lanuginosum between rocks

carpet of mosses
Dicranum
Polytrichum
Rhytidiadelphus
Plagiochila
(a liverwort)

The burned heath

Heathlands have thin peaty or sandy soil. They often have low rainfall, especially in the summer, and become very dry. Heathers, gorse, bracken, and wiry grasses cover the heath. On the ground, there is a layer of the previous year's dry bracken fronds. Fires are a real danger in midsummer. Sometimes these are spontaneous (occur naturally), but more often they are caused by careless picnickers or cigarette butts. Heathland shrubs have tiny leaves or spines and they burn very readily. It only takes a few minutes for the heath to be blackened. The first colonizers of burned ground are mosses (see below). In time, all the other heathland flowers and shrubs return.

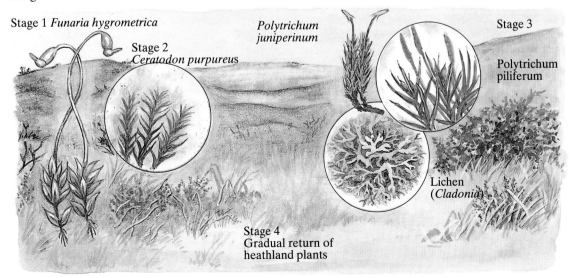

Stage 1 *Funaria hygrometrica*

Stage 2
Ceratodon purpureus

Polytrichum juniperinum

Stage 3

Polytrichum piliferum

Lichen (*Cladonia*)

Stage 4
Gradual return of heathland plants

A WORLD IN MINIATURE

In spite of their small size, mosses and liverworts are very variable and are able to live in many different habitats. The shape they take depends on the way they grow. Mosses only grow from the tips of their shoots. Patches or clumps of moss may consist of an enormous number of separate plants, or a tuft of plants may arise from many buds on one protonema. Creeping mats of mosses or liverworts are impossible to untangle into separate plants.

Down at moss level, even small changes in the environment are important. Most woodland mosses prefer still, damp places. Yet within one corner of the woods, the tiny differences in the environment of a tree trunk, the base of the tree, and a rotting log mean that different groups of bryophytes are found on them. Damp woods are very good places to hunt for lots of different sorts of mosses and liverworts.

Beside a mountain stream

Mountain streams gurgle and splash over a jumble of rocks (see below). Trickles of water that seep down a rock face keep the surface wet all year round, as well as washing nutrients down from above. Large patches of liverworts such as *Marsupella emarginata* and *Scapania undulata*, and mosses such as *Brachythecium rivulare*, *Dicranella palustris* and *Hyocomium flagellare* grow side by side, frequently in places where flowering plants do not manage to grow.

The tree trunk

The most important features of a tree trunk as far as the growth of mosses is concerned is the aspect and texture of the trunk. Trees or bushes with a rough bark, for example oaks, ashes, and elders, are more likely to be mossy than trees with smooth barks. However, the covering of epiphytes is not the same all the way around the tree trunk. The side exposed to wind and sun dries out quickly. This stops the growth of many mosses, but is ideal for lichens. Most mosses are seen on the shadiest, dampest side of the trunk.

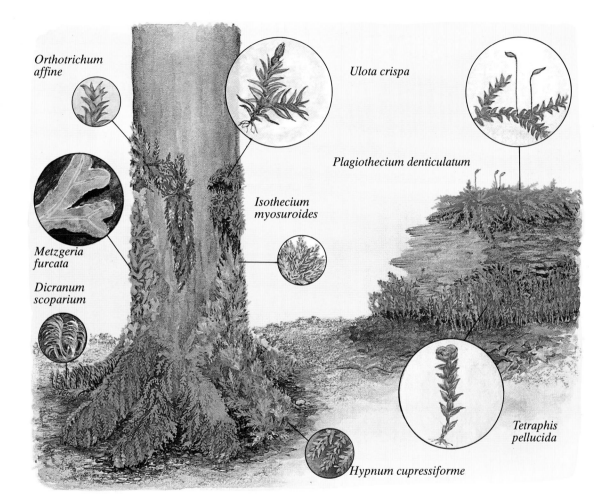

Orthotrichum affine

Ulota crispa

Plagiothecium denticulatum

Isothecium myosuroides

Metzgeria furcata

Dicranum scoparium

Tetraphis pellucida

Hypnum cupressiforme

The base of the tree

The base of a tree is less exposed than the trunk to the drying effects of the wind and sun. Often leafy plants and ferns cast a shade, and the ground itself gives off moisture. So the mossy "sock" around the base of the tree is especially luxuriant. It is also richer in nutrients because dead leaves and soil get trapped around the tree roots and animals such as mice and squirrels leave their droppings. Mosses that need more fertile surroundings all thrive here.

Rotting wood

A rotting log may seem an unpromising site for a nature study, but it is teeming with a variety of plants and animals. Inside there are wood-rotting fungi and wood-boring beetles, as well as woodlice, earwigs, spiders, mites – all enclosed in a soft, damp world of pulpy wood. On the outside of the log is a thick layer of mosses, which help to keep it moist. Nutrients, essential for the growth of mosses, seep from the decaying log.

LIFE IN A BOG OR SWAMP

Bogmosses are home to many animals and plants, including tussocky grasses, sedges, and rushes and a few flowering plants. These can all grow in waterlogged conditions, and survive on very poor, infertile land. Nutrients containing nitrogen and phosphorus are in very short supply. To overcome this, some bogplants have become **insectivorous**.

Plants cannot chase their prey, so they have to trap the insects instead (see below). Without the original mosses, these unique habitats would not have developed, and neither would the plants and animals they contain. Many bogs are threatened. If they disappear, not only will the original bogmosses be lost but all the other plants and animals will be endangered.

The insectivores

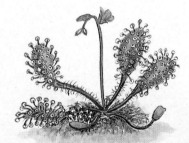

Sundews have leaves with long, sticky hairs. They glisten and shine, attracting small flies. Once an insect lands on the leaf, it is stuck and cannot get free. The leaf slowly folds up, producing chemicals that digest the insect. The vital nutrients can then be absorbed by the plant.

Bladderworts are water plants. They live in small pools with only the flower stems above the water. On each spray of leaves there is a small bladder, which is tightly closed when empty. When a tiny water creature brushes against sensitive hairs at the opening, a "trap door" opens inward. As water rushes in, the animal is sucked in, too.

Butterworts have sticky leaves. They are a pale yellowish green. When an insect is caught, the edges of the leaves curl over it, preventing its escape.

Pitcher plants are native to North America, but they are also very much at home in Irish bogs. The leaves form deep "pitchers," with a slippery rim and digestive juices at the bottom. Insects landing on the rim fall in and cannot get out.

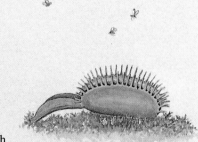

The Venus flytrap is a rare plant of swamps in North and South Carolina. When an insect lands, sensitive hairs act as triggers and the spiny leaf snaps shut.

Sphagnum swamps of the eastern United States

Along the coastal plains of the eastern U.S., there were once vast areas of swamps. Many of these have been drained. Fortunately, some areas, for example Dismal Swamp (Va. – N.C.) and Okefenokee Swamp (Ga.), are now protected as national wildlife reserves (see right). These swamps have areas of wet woodland, marsh, and sphagnum. Both abound with wildlife, especially amphibians, birds, reptiles, and insects.

Tupelo, silver and red maples, and swamp cypresses grow in Dismal Swamp. The endangered bog turtle lives in the sphagnum bogs and slow-flowing streams. It has become scarce because so much of its habitat has been drained and developed. The Okefenokee Swamp has a subtropical climate, and has a rich mixture of plants and animals.

The American alligator

This large reptile inhabits the coastal plains of the southeastern U.S. from North Carolina to Florida and Texas. The Okefenokee Swamp is toward the northern part of its range. In the 1960s, the numbers of this alligator had fallen so low that it was put on the endangered animals list. Alligator hunting was stopped, and areas of its wetland habitat were made into wildlife reserves. Its populations recovered quickly, and it is no longer at risk. Today there are about 6,000 alligators in the Okefenokee Swamp alone.

THREATENED BOGS

Organisms that break down or decompose dead material cannot work well in a bog or swamp. First, it is too wet, so there is not enough oxygen. Second, it is very acidic. Third, water evaporates from the surface of the bog all the time so that the water stays cool, even in summer. This means that bacteria and fungi grow and multiply very slowly. As more and more dead plant remains build up on the surface, the lower layers become squashed into solid peat. The layer of peat increases in thickness by about .075 inch a year. This process may continue for thousands of years. Some bogs in Britain are 7,000 years old, and some in North America are 9,000 years or more old.

domestic fuel

industrial fuel

plant compost

peat flowerpots

mushroom compost

Uses of peat

Peat is a traditional domestic fuel in countries such as Ireland, western Scotland, Finland, and the Soviet Union. Small-scale peat cutting is not a great threat to the bogs. However, peat extraction has now become an important industry in many countries, with new developments starting up in places like New Zealand and Chile as the demand for horticultural peat increases. The Soviet Union has 76 peat-fueled power stations. In Ireland, peat has been cut on a huge scale since the 1950s and is also used in power stations.

In the 1980s, conservationists from Ireland itself, Britain, and Holland became alarmed at the rate the Irish bogs were disappearing. Some areas have since been made into nature reserves, but the Irish Peatland Conservation Society still fears for the future of Ireland's unspoiled bogs. If the commercial peat cutting continues unabated, Irish peat reserves will have been exhausted soon after the year 2000. A valuable habitat, and all the animals and plants in it, will have been lost unless the demand for peat can be drastically reduced.

Peat cutting

Peat for domestic use was once cut by hand. It still is in rural areas, but it is hard, slow work. A small ditch is dug for excess water to drain away, and blocks of peat called turfs are sliced out. The peat turfs are stacked under shelters to dry out.

Before peat is cut commercially, large, long ditches are excavated across the bog with heavy machines (see right). Then, peat intended for power stations is removed in giant peat "sausages" by other machines. Peat for the horticultural industry is scraped off after the surface vegetation has been cleared and then removed by machines like enormous vacuum cleaners.

World peat bogs

About 1 percent of the land surface of the world is peat bog. The largest areas are in Russia, but North America, and northwest Europe also have important peat bogs. Sphagnum bogs are just one kind of wetland that are threatened worldwide by drainage or pollution. In the U.S., much of the naturally swampy land of the eastern coastal plain has been drained for agriculture, forestry, or building and development. These unique swamps, which took thousands of years to form, and all the life forms that depend on them are being destroyed and lost forever.

GUIDES TO POLLUTION

Increasing industrialization, together with the huge expansion of car ownership, has meant that pollutants of all kinds have been released into the air, soil, and water. Metal-ore furnaces, or smelters, incinerated wastes, and car exhausts are principal sources of heavy-metal pollution. Some of these metals are very toxic to people and animals. High levels of lead can be damaging to children, affecting their ability to learn.

Experts can tell a lot about the air and soil from the growth of mosses. Many are very sensitive to sulfur dioxide pollution, which is why few are found in large cities. The appearance of many different sorts indicates clean air. Some species will only grow on certain soils or rocks. *Pleurozium* or *Rhacomitrium* only grow on acid ground. *Ditrichum flexicaule* and *Encalypta streptocarpa* grow on chalk.

Heavy-metal pollution

Heavy metals are elements such as lead, cadmium, nickel, zinc, copper, or mercury. Small amounts occur naturally in the environment and are no cause for concern. Indeed, some, like copper and zinc, are essential to animal health in very small quantities. Some, however, are very harmful to animals and plants. The diagram below shows how heavy metals from various sources can pollute the air.

How metals enter the air we breathe

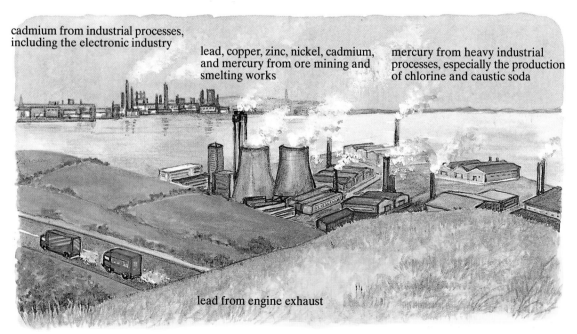

cadmium from industrial processes, including the electronic industry

lead, copper, zinc, nickel, cadmium, and mercury from ore mining and smelting works

mercury from heavy industrial processes, especially the production of chlorine and caustic soda

lead from engine exhaust

Lead in gasoline

A chemical called lead tetra-ethyl was first put into gas in 1923. It is often called an "anti-knock agent" because it makes the car engine run more smoothly. Lead bromide comes out in the car's exhaust, together with other waste gases. Concern about the quantities of lead being put into the environment began in the early 1960s, when it was discovered that the soil of road shoulders contained over 150 times the normal level of lead!

Plants growing beside roads also contained too much lead. Mosses had the highest level of all, because they naturally absorb minerals from the air through their leaves. For a long time people were unwilling to accept that car exhaust was responsible for lead pollution or that it was harmful.

Ore smelters

By the 1960s, scientists found the environment around smelting works was so polluted that mosses could not grow. To measure the amounts of metals released into the air, they devised "moss bags" (see right). Sphagnum and *Hypnum* mosses were put into net bags. These were put up in the areas under study, and any heavy metals were absorbed into the moss leaves. Back in the laboratory, the amounts absorbed were measured to find the level of pollution.

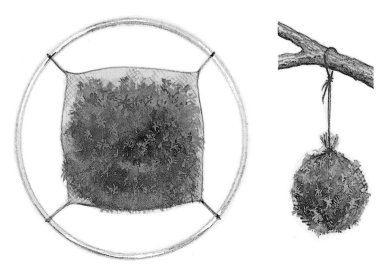

UNRAVELING THE PAST

Studying peat bogs and the plant and animal remains they contain can tell us a lot about the past. For example, many pollen grains are found, produced by flowering plants and the cones of fir and spruce trees. The outer layer of the pollen grain is very tough and resistant to decay, so pollen that lands on a peat bog decays very little. Pollen grains often have a distinctive shape or surface pattern that an expert can use to tell which plant released it.

Human history

Peat bogs have also preserved valuable remains of human settlements and cultures – and even bodies (see right). Buried in wet peat, the lack of oxygen and high acidity has meant that the corpses have virtually been pickled! These relics have been discovered during peat cutting. Important finds have been made in Ireland, Denmark, and Britain. Some of the earliest are from the Middle Stone Age, about 8,600 years ago, and are mostly flint tools.

Iron Age tribes in Denmark often buried people in bogs. Archaeologists uncovering these bodies have been able to tell a lot about life at that time. They can even tell what these ancient peoples had eaten before they died, because their stomach contents were so well preserved! Learning about the diet and clothing of these bygone cultures has added greatly to our understanding of early human history.

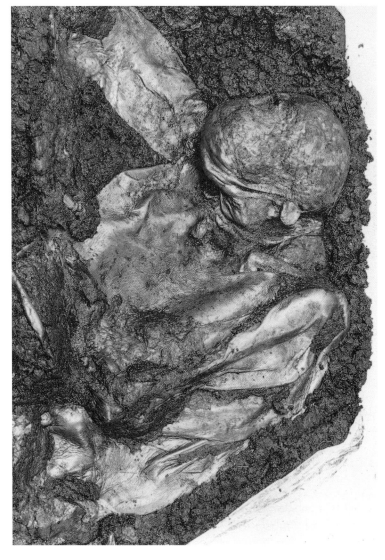

The oldest peat is at the bottom of the bog. Samples taken at various levels can be treated with chemicals to separate the pollen. Identifying it tells scientists what plants were growing around the bog throughout its long history. This information helps construct a picture of past climates. For instance, a lot of pine and birch pollen indicates a cool climate similar to that of the conifer forests of today. A lot of oak, hazel, and hornbeam pollen means that the climate was warmer.

Treasure trove

In Ireland, "bog hoards" are collections of items hidden by people. No one is sure whether people buried their possessions deliberately or they were accidentally lost. Some of the Bronze Age hoards recovered contain the remains of woven baskets and household utensils, but others are finely made bronze tools or gold jewelry. Later hoards dating from about AD 1000 contain beautiful gold and silver vessels from early monasteries. No doubt peat bogs in many parts of the world still hide treasures.

The antiseptic moss

Sphagnum is probably the only moss used by people to any great extent. Its enormous powers of absorption, together with the acidity that makes it naturally antiseptic, have meant that it has been used for dressing wounds as recently as World War I. It has also been used as diapers. Today, it is thought that it could be useful for mopping up small oil spills in the sea.

43

GLOSSARY

ANTHERIDIUM (plural antheridia) – The male reproductive organ of a moss or liverwort that produces male sex cells.

ARCHEGONIUM (plural archegonia) – The female reproductive organ of a moss or liverwort that produces a single female sex cell.

AXIL – The angle between the upper surface of the leaf or leaf-stalk and the stem.

BRYOLOGIST – A person who studies mosses and liverworts.

BRYOPHYTES – The group of plants consisting of mosses and liverworts.

CALYPTRA – The remains of the archegonium that make a thin cap over the tip of the moss capsule.

CAPSULE – The part of the sporophyte that contains the spores.

CHLOROPHYLL – The green pigment in plants that uses the energy in sunlight to make food by photosynthesis.

CUTICLE – A waxy waterproof layer covering the surface of some liverworts and mosses and most other plants.

ECTOHYDRIC – Mosses and liverworts that absorb water through their leaves.

ENDOHYDRIC – Mosses and liverworts that absorb water through their rhizoids.

EPIPHYTE – A plant that grows on another plant.

FERTILIZE – To fuse a male sex cell with a female to form a new individual.

FLAGELLA – Minute hairs that enable gametes and microorganisms to swim.

GAMETES – The male and female sex cells.

GAMETOPHYTE – The stage in a plant's life cycle that bears the male and female sex organs.

GEMMA (plural gemmae) – Small, budlike growths that can grow into new moss or liverwort plants.

GENERATIONS – The gametophyte and sporophyte stages in the life cycles of mosses and liverworts.

HABITAT – The natural home of a plant or animal.

INSECTIVOROUS – Plants or animals that eat insects.

NICHE – The mini-environments that make up a bog, swamp, forest, or tundra where conditions are just right for particular plants or animals.

PEAT – The compressed, dead but unrotted remains of bog plants.

PERIANTH – The petals of a flowering plant and the leaves enclosing the archegonium of a liverwort.

PERISTOME – The ring of moisture-sensitive teeth around the mouth of a moss capsule.

PERMAFROST – Ground that is always frozen, even in summer.

PHOTOSYNTHESIS – The process in chlorophyll-containing plants that uses sunlight to convert carbon dioxide gas and water into sugars, releasing oxygen.

POLYGONS – The many-sided shapes seen on the ground of the tundra, made by the repeated freezing and thawing of the soil surface.

PRIMARY COLONIZERS – The kinds of plants that are the first to grow on bare ground.

PROTONEMA – The small plantlet first formed when a bryophyte spore germinates.

RHIZOIDS – Very simple threadlike growths that mosses and liverworts have instead of roots.

SETA – The thin stalk that is part of the sporophyte of most mosses and liverworts.

SEXUAL REPRODUCTION – The way living things increase in number by combining sex cells from different individuals to make new individuals.

SPORE – Minute powdery units produced by non-flowering plants that can grow into new plants.

SPOROPHYTE – The stage of a plant's life cycle that produces the spores.

STABILIZE – To fix something so that it does not move or blow about.

SUCCESSION – A series of plants that grow one after the other in a disturbed environment.

THALLUS – A plant body that is not organized into stem and leaves.

TUNDRA – Cold polar regions of north and south where only low-growing plants can live.

WEFT – A loose, spreading network of creeping stems.

ZOOSPORE – A spore that has flagella and so can swim through water.

FURTHER READING

For children
Secrets of a Salt Marsh by John Snow; Gannett, no date.
For adults
Encyclopedia of Horticulture by Thomas H. Everett; Garland, 1981.
The Encyclopedia of the Plant Kingdom edited by Anthony Huxley; Chartwell, 1977.
How to Know the Mosses & Liverworts 2nd ed., by Henry S. Conrad and Paul Redfern; Wm. C. Brown, 1979.

BRYOPHYTES IN THIS BOOK

Mosses
Andreaea (mountain moss)
Andreaea rupestris
Anthoceros (hornwort)
Aulacomnium palustre
Bogmoss or sphagnum (*Sphagnum* species:
    S. capillifolium; S. cuspidatum;
    S. magellanicum; S. papillosum; S. rubellum)
Brachythecium rivulare
Brachythecium rutabulum
Bryum argenteum
Bryum pendulum
Cephaloziella arctica
Ceratodon purpureus
Cinclidotus fontinaloides
Cirriphyllum crassinervium
Climacium dendroides
Dawsonia species (*D. superba*)
Dicranella heteromalla
Dicranella palustris
Dicranum species (*D. scoparium*)
Distichium capillaceum
Ditrichum flexicaule
Drepanocladus uncinatus
Encalypta streptocarpa
Eurynchium praelongum
Eurynchium riparoides = Rhynchostegium
    riparoides
Fissidens species (*F. adianthoides*)
Fontinalis antipyretica
Funaria species (*F. hygrometrica*)
Grimmia species (*G. maritima; G. pulvinata*)
Hookeria lucens
Hylocomium splendens
Hyocomium flagellare
Hypnum species (*H. cupressiforme*)
Isopterygium elegans
Isothecium myosuroides
Leucobryum species (*L. glaucum*)
Mnium species (*M. hornum*)
Mountain mosses (*Andreaea* species)
Neohodgsonia mirabilis
Orthotrichum affine
Orthotrichum diaphanum

Plagiothecium denticulatum
Pleurozium species (*P. schreberi*)
Polytrichum species (*P. commune; P. juniperinum;*
    P. piliferum)
Pseudoscleropodium purum
Pterobryella papuensis
Pulchrinodus inflatus
Rhacomitrium species (*R. canescens;*
    R. lanuginosum)
Rhynchostegium species (*R. confertum;*
    R. serratum)
Rhytidiadelphus species (*R. squarrosus*)
Seligeria calcarea
Spiridens
Splachnum
Tetraphis pellucida
Thuidium tamariscinum
Tortula muralis
Tortula ruraliformis
Ulota crispa
Ulota phyllantha

LIVERWORTS
Thallose
Conocephalum conicum
Lunularia cruciata
Marchantia species (*M. polymorpha*)
Metzgeria furcata
Riccia species (*R. fluitans*)

Leafy
Bazzania trilobata
Frullania dilatata
Marsupella emarginata
Lophocolea heterophylla
Lophozia
Plagiochila species (*P. asplenioides*)
Porella platyphylla
Scapania undulata

INDEX